Supernatural Eve

What is a miracle, anyway? It is an extraordinary event manifesting a supernatural work of God. It is up to us to credit God with these events or not. I consider it a miracle when I lose my husband in a group of thousands, and I ask God to find him. I turn around and there he is! Did God move me to pray at that moment? Perhaps. Is that a miracle? Money is short and on paper there is not nearly enough to pay the bills. God is praised for His goodness, and the bills get paid. Is it a miracle? You decide.

If you know God, you know how wonderful He is, and all He has done for you. He is so good to those that trust Him. A friend came with a broken arm to our weekly Bible study, and we prayed for her. That day, her doctor took an x-ray of her arm and removed the cast because the break had completely healed in just a few days! He was amazed and so was she.

We had a great camping weekend planned. Both families were relieved that none caught the virus filling the hospitals. Then our friend Roy came down suddenly with all the symptoms, a severe headache and fever, right after we set up the tents. Fear gripped us until it dawned on us God is the healer. A few minutes after we prayed, Roy got up and came in the room, perfectly well! None of us got sick, and we had a wonderful time. How amazing it was to ask, expect, but then to see it happen before our eyes!

God healed my back years ago from lower back pain following a trampoline injury when I was a teen. I couldn't stand straight when I was stressed out, and had to walk bent over or go to bed a couple weeks. I became a Christian. The next week a new friend explained salvation includes health, and she prayed for me. She said to just thank Jesus no matter how I felt, and the pain would go away. I moved furniture that night, in terrible pain, but had to do it, with company coming for Thanksgiving dinner the next day. I kept saying, "Lord, thank you for healing me!" as I crawled around. I went to bed and slept fitfully. It seemed worse than ever. But I kept thanking God through the night. I woke in the morning, healed

Jesus healed my mom from the Asian flu during an epidemic. He instantly healed her as a 700 Club counselor prayed with me on the phone. She called my house in the morning saying, "I got a miracle! All of a sudden, my pain went away!" I asked what time she got better, and it was the very moment we were praying on the phone.

The list of miracles would fill many books, over forty years of them. Some are documented with medical records, such as my husband's blind spots. He is diabetic, and could not drive at night because of broken blood vessels, mostly in one eye. He went to the elders of the church who anointed him with oil and prayed a prayer of faith. The doctor is still amazed that God healed his eye and also gave him twenty-twenty vision in that eye, which he never had!

One time I had an ingrown toenail, and the pain was just awful. I was one huge toe! All I could think of was the pain! I suffered a whole day and night. At 3 A.M. the Lord spoke inside me and said, "Just praise Me." (For this pain? It sounded ludicrous!) As soon as I began to thank and praise Jesus, within ten minutes I was healed! I never had another. It was a good lesson for me. It is astounding what prayer can do. What an awesome God we have! He hears it all.

On the way to college on a four-lane highway, I was too closely following a huge dump truck in the center lane. The road was clear ice. Suddenly the truck braked, and I kept going! I screamed, "Jesus!"

My car instantly moved sideways into the next lane tightly squeezed between two vehicles, still moving forward at the same speed, and the steering wheel never turned. As soon as possible, I got off the road, and parked on the shoulder trembling in shock, but so thankful.

Another time, I was towing a large houseboat through the Tennessee Mountains from Michigan to Georgia. I was unaware my father's trailer was not strong enough to support a boat of that size, and halfway down the mountain, one of the trailer axles cracked! The tire flew over the car, and my son and I were tossed around as the car and trailer whipped back and forth toward a cliff. I screamed, "Jesus!" The car jerked to a halt after the car swerved into the median, just as traffic veered around the corner. God answered every prayer for the next few days in astounding ways. We got the boat home in perfect condition after twenty-three miracles. It is published in "Heaven Touching Earth" by James Stuart Bell.

So often I weep with pure joy. I can hardly wait to get alone and tell the Lord everything about my day, and I sit and listen to Him speak to me. He seems to communicate with us all in different ways. He gives my friend visions! He always speaks things that are in the Bible.

Table of Contents

Chapter One: Miracles
Miracles in the Bush	8
A Fiery Exit	17
Miracle Landing	25
Come Here, Boy	28
Two Turn Away Ten Thousand	30

Chapter Two: Angelic Encounters
The Dead Guy	33
A Light in the Darkness	37

Chapter Three Deliverance and Cults
We are more than Conquerors	40
Why do we Hurt Ourselves	46
The Grail Movement	52
The Bread of Life	55
Women's Aglow	59

Chapter Four: Finding Jesus
A Gift of Miracles	61
This Little Light of Mine	66
The Most Spectacular Miracle	71

Chapter Five: Dreams and Visions
I Loved Donuts	75
Last Chance	90
A Peek into Tomorrow	95
The Green Men	100
An EMP Dream	104
Visions	107
A Message from the Holy Spirit	113

For verily I say unto you, That whosoever shall say unto this mountain, Be thou removed, and be thou cast into the sea; and shall not doubt in his heart, but shall believe that those things which he saith shall come to pass; he shall have whatsoever he saith. ²⁴ Therefore I say unto you, What things soever ye desire, when ye pray, believe that ye receive them, and ye shall have them. **Mark 11:23-24 (KJV)**

I know your hearts will rejoice when you realize these stories are evidence of God's enormous love for His children. See if you can make up questions that follow each story, and use them in Bible studies and Sunday school classes. Jesus told stories to teach lessons, and we can as well.

Chapter One
Miracle Stories

Miracles in the Bush
By Eric A.

I must first explain some things that went on in Ghana, Africa, around 1994. A land conflict between the Ethnic groups of Konkombas and Nunumbas resulted in the "Guinea Fowl War" in north-eastern Ghana. Ancient conflicts ignited after a discussion on a market place. Up to 2000 were killed and 150,000 displaced. A peace treaty was signed, but violence broke out again several times in the following years.

Born in Ghana, I am the firstborn of eight children, an only son with seven girls. I had a beautiful mother, who was my dear friend. My dad grew up as a seaman and had become very rich; he was also the son of an African king, a prince. He had much gold, which is good, but can be a magnet for trouble. When Ghana suffered a revolution, people, especially those that had money or influence were killed first; they were slaughtered everywhere. When we were still able to get out safely, to preserve our lives, we moved from Ghana to Liberia, which is like moving from Savannah to Atlanta, about six hours away.

Soon after we arrived, Liberia fell into a recession. The Canadian government hired some people, which included me, to run a research program called IDLC. They gave us $160,000 to run the program, which was good money in those days. This enabled us to help victims of the war. Prisons were deplorable, overcrowded, with inadequate food, no fresh water, no bedding unless relatives supply it, and bare floors to sleep on. Some do not even have clothes to wear. Because Liberia ended up at war as well as Ghana, we were again in danger. Any time there is war there are demons. War is hell. Without God, who could bear it?

When the enemy comes in like a flood, the Lord raises up a standard against him. God sent us a wonderful influential woman. Michelle Smith from the Lighthouse church in Oklahoma came to us with her prophetic gift. God poured so many gifts into her. She became to us like a mother or sister, and encouraged all the believers. She even talked with the president of Liberia before she came back to America. When the war started she prophesied to me, "You are going through the war but out of it you will have a double portion, an increase." She took us to a plane and gave me some money and we went back home to Ghana.

A prophetic friend and I were praying in my home when my wife came in the room saying, "A stranger is at the door and needs food." Almost everyone needed food. Shops were closed. Banks were closed. Markets were closed. Everything was being looted. "Share what we have," I said to my wife, but I didn't really want to. We had two children, Duke and Prize, and needed what we had left. I only offered it to show off my generosity in front of our guest.

She walked out but came right back in. I looked at her worried face. "He also wants ten dollars." We had some U.S. dollars, which were rare at that time. Prices had gone sky high but even then there was no place to get any food. What had been 50 cents was now $5 if anyone was willing to sell. It was good for the stranger that our guest was there, because I confess, that hour I simply didn't have that much faith. She gave it to the man and he left. After my friend went home I blamed her for everything! It was so wrong of me. She was just doing what I had told her to do.

Six days later someone knocked loudly at my door. I was reading my Bible-nothing else to do in those days. There stood this scary looking man with a mask over his face and a bag in his hands. I shivered, feeling like the devil was standing right there in front of me. He just stood there and made a strange sound muffled through the mask. I cried, "Jesus!"

Surprised, he dropped his bag, pulled that thing off his ugly scarred face, and looking to my wife, shocked her by saying, "I came to thank you! You saved my life that day. I had fallen into a fire on my face!" I saw inside the bag he had dropped. He had a human head in the bag! "You gave me food and I am grateful," he said. Here was a fighting rebel thanking us! I realized that act of giving saved our lives. He might have killed us all if we had not given it freely. We had no idea God had again saved our lives.

The war intensified. It was very difficult for my wife to remain unafraid. Someone ran to the door and said, "Pack up! You have thirty minutes to leave. Go now!" It reminded me of the message an angel gave Lot in Sodom. My wife Edith thought we would come back. That is the only reason she was able to pack so quickly! She took only what we needed.

We took money with us that would keep us for a while. We went behind the rebel lines. Life was extremely different. We never did get back to our wonderful home. We had to fend for ourselves along with thousands of people. Many were killed. Only seventeen of us came out of it without a scratch. That was a very small number. We saw and experienced awful things that we cannot talk about even today.

A man told us to escape into the bush, where we spent the next two and a half years! God led us to water or we would have all perished. My wife's grandmother joined us there, but she died from the difficult situation. She was 82. It was horrible in the bush. We put palm branches over us and had an old cassette radio with a few batteries. I put the batteries in the sun to increase their energy to listen to just one more broadcast. We heard that soon the war would be over. It wasn't.

One day some Christian people came and found me in the bush and brought me to pray for someone. I arrived to find a dead woman! God led me to pray that she would return to life and she did! Many miracles occurred during this time. This was the first of several people that returned to life in answer to our prayers. God was a present help in times of need. He answered us and poured His Spirit out to strengthen us, meeting our needs daily. We didn't have all our wants, but God provided for our survival.

Soon after this event, while still living in the bush, three-year-old Prize had just stopped crying when we heard footsteps walking toward us. A group of rebels appeared suddenly, fully armed. They were furious to find me there-or just furious for any reason. The leader shoved his face close to mine. "What are you doing here?" he yelled. I knew very well what they do to people, and my heart raced. Accusing me, he said, "You don't fight in the front?"

It is amazing how quickly we can lie. "I am praying for you! This is what I do for a living-pray for people. This is my lifestyle. I am in the bush praying for the good work you are doing," I lied.

He saw my Bible and radio. He carried a bottle of gin. He opened a bullet, and poured what I assumed was lead from the bullet into the gin bottle! It crossed my mind this red-eyed maniac was going to test my praying ability by making me drink it! Perhaps God intervened at that point because instead he drank it right in front of me! Then he took something from his pocket and showed it to me. Opium!

"Ah," I said. "It's in the Bible-herbs!" Another test? Why he showed it to me I did not know, so I quickly changed the subject. I asked if I could pray for them all, right then - good timing, eh? "Don't close your eyes. I will close my eyes," I said. I prayed in the Spirit. He didn't know what I was saying but God did. After the prayer, I said, "You will leave now, and in three days you will be promoted." To my great relief, they left!

I had no idea I was really speaking from God but weeks later the rebel leader ran into me again. "What you told me happened just like you said it would, and I got promoted!" He was overjoyed to see me, calling me "God-man", giving me food and money and asking me to pray for all his men, which, of course, I did, even though I was not on the side of the rebels. (God always seeks to save the lost.)

In the meantime, my wife began getting very heavy and swollen, but it didn't dawn on me for some time that a baby was on the way! I probably didn't want to imagine it in the bush. During the pregnancy we had again been confronted with death. Rebels were ready to shoot me, and I pleaded with them to let us live because Edith, standing there, was about to have a baby and she needed me. God moved on their hearts and they turned and left us alone! The prophecy from Michelle was right. We were increasing- just not the way I expected.

A while later, I was out seeking food and was again surrounded by heavily armed rebels, with knives drawn to slit my throat. I was quite concerned this time and tried not to fear them, talking fast, but it was not looking good for me. The leader gave a command and they all mobbed me while I pleaded for my life. Suddenly the leader said, "Stop! You just said my mother's name! Are you the man who raised her from the dead?"

"Yes!" I cried joyfully, in great relief. I told the man all about the event, convincing him it was true.

"This man is not to be touched! He is a holy man." God saved me again! It was no coincidence that this particular woman was raised. How did her name even come about? They left me alone, trembling but rejoicing!

In a short time, I was able to send my family to America. Later I joined them, God had called me long before to become a pastor. I worked first as a janitor at Landmark Church in Norcross, Georgia, and over time became the associate pastor before God gave me a small church congregation of my own. God has met all our needs through His riches in glory through Christ Jesus, our Savior!

God knows where we are going from birth to death. We will build a testimony if we walk His walk. We are soldiers of Christ. It will not be easy. Anyone who says this is going to be easy is lying. God will perform for you and show you great and mighty things. This is about what God can do for all of us. He is no respecter of persons.

Numbers 23:19 (KJV) *God is not a man, that he should lie; neither the son of man, that he should repent: hath he said, and shall he not do it? Or hath he spoken, and shall he not make it good?*

If we can realize that God the Father is not a man, we will understand so many more things. Man is not like God. Man lies. Man repents. Man will die. God does not die.

Job 5:12 (KJV) *He disappoints the devices of the crafty, so that their hands cannot perform their enterprise.*

He performs great and mighty things for you. He said when you walk in the valley of the shadow of death He will be with you. **Isaiah 41:13 (KJV)**

The Crabby King

"Off with their heads!" Sounds like Alice in Wonderland, but it was true! If they couldn't tell him what he dreamed, they would lose their lives. How unrealistic.

The king of Babylon, we will call Neb for short, had a dream that he had forgotten but it still bothered him. He called his wise men and asked them to interpret it. They asked him to tell what the dream was, but he couldn't. He decided to kill them all in his fury over their obviously deceiving ways, figuring out they would make something up if they heard it. He decided if they were really powerful in the spirit realm, they could have told him the dream.

The four Jews that had been captured and put to work in the palace were included in this mass murder decree. After the four had sought God for an answer, God actually gave one of them,

Daniel, the dream. He quickly went to the guard in charge and asked to see the king.

He told the king what he had dreamed and God gave Daniel the interpretation, which puffed up the king pretty good. His power went to his head.

As a result, King Neb built for his subjects a huge golden statue of himself, a hundred twenty-five feet high! He had all the leaders assembled to celebrate the dedication of the image. A herald ordered everyone to bow, falling on their faces, to the statue when the music began to play. Everyone, of course, fell before it, except three men. Daniel must have been out of town. He was not mentioned.

Some jealous Chaldeans (who probably didn't want to bow either) came to the kind and tattled on Shadrach, Meshach and Abednego. "They didn't bow to your image, Sir!" The king immediately had them arrested and brought before him.

"Is this accusation true?" he asked. He gave them a second chance to fall on their faces by starting up the music again, but they just stood there. He got furious! He demanded an answer and warned them they would be destroyed in a furnace if they didn't answer as he wanted.

"Our God is able to deliver us and he will. But if not, we will not serve your gods or bow to the image. Neb was beside himself with fury. "Heat that fire seven times hotter than usual and throw them in!"

A group of soldiers bound them with all their clothes on and threw them into the fiery furnace, which was so hot the fire burned up the soldiers!

The king looked into the furnace and was astonished to see not three, but four men, unbound, walking around inside the huge furnace! "One looks like a son of a god!" he cried. "Come out of there!"

The fire had no power over them, not even leaving the smell of smoke on their clothing. The king said, "Blessed be the God of Shadrach, Meshach and Abednego, who sent his angel and delivered those that trusted him!"

He made a decree that everyone that speaks against the God of these men will be cut into pieces and their houses be made a dunghill, because there is no other God that can deliver after this way. Then he promoted them.

God delivers people from fires in our day also. It may not be quite as profound to you, but I bet Ollie thought so when his ordeal was all over. God is the same today, yesterday, and forever. The story is found in Daniel 3:1-30.

A Fiery Exit

Have you ever seen a house collapse flat to the ground right before your eyes? That is what the neighbors saw when Ollie's house blew up. He was shot right through the wall of the house, between the studs, taking the chunks of plaster lathe right out with him! All they could see was a fireball flying onto the lawn. Ollie was on fire from head to toe.

What happens to skin when polyester pants light up is not a pretty sight. The fibers weave themselves into the body like glue. But God was with Ollie, putting up one barrier after another to protect him. He flew out of the wall, left with only his belt, pants pockets and jacket. The pants had completely dissolved before they could embed into his legs.

In this most astounding intervention, God orchestrated the whole rescue from start to finish.

Now you might say, "Why did God let it happen in the first place?" He does not interrupt every tragedy the world gets itself into, but for His children, He moves even the stars in the heavens if necessary. God loves us more than we will ever imagine. He does not want us in pain. If He did, He never would have sent Jesus to die on a cross to give us an escape from hell.

Ollie trusted Jesus so long now he can't remember when he didn't. Some say you must know the date you were born again, but many are saved as little children before they scarcely even need forgiveness. God protected him from death all his life, and he made it triumphantly seventy-seven years so far. He doesn't know of a day that God's Spirit has not been actively walking with him.

Several years ago, Ollie decided to put city water in his house and connect to a city sewer, which required digging a trench in his front yard. Ray, his plumber, hired a man to dig the trench, but no one noticed the backhoe operator was drunk. Circumstances came together to create a disaster. A nearby factory had shut down, but the gas lines that supplied it were still under pressure, and led also to Ollie's property.

The inebriated driver didn't notice the small warning flags posted on the ground to keep this very thing from happening. As he dug the trench he accidentally hooked and pulled up the gas-filled line. Ollie had just entered the basement to turn off his own line at the very moment an enormous supply of gas gushed into his furnace. The furnace instantly exploded, lighting him on fire as a huge fireball worked its way up the stairwell, shooting the human cannonball right through the plaster and out of the house, shattering the cedar siding as he slammed into it.

Ollie felt time slow down, and watched in fascination as each event played out in front of him. He was just a passive participant at this point, and did nothing but stare as he watched flames flow over him. His nylon jacket melted to his body, the cotton lining insulating him from the fire. The only parts of him on fire were his legs, face and hands. Thirty-two percent of his body received third-degree burns, meaning all the skin was burned off, as well as damaging and destroying tender nerve endings.

Meanwhile, his wife and daughter were still in the house, which rose up as the entire house flew off the foundation. An upright grand piano was covered with Ollie's bowling trophies, and a marble trophy soared into Beth's head, requiring stitches. She could easily have been killed as those trophies flew around the room, but God had His angels at work.

One might say, "Why did she get hurt at all?" If she had not been hit, she and her child would have reached the front door and been crushed to death as the house came down and landed in the basement. Instead, they walked out through the hole made by Ollie's fiery body just as the house collapsed behind them. It was all over in seven minutes!

Ollie's story is amazing. Not a bone was broken during his flight from the basement. His glasses remained on! His recovery in the burns center at the hospital was remarkable. The process of removing dead tissue after severe burns is terribly painful, but not once did he even cry out, which if you have ever gone through such a thing, you understand this is nearly impossible, except for God's grace and mercy. He knows the profound power of rejoicing in his tribulations.

He listened to God. At the hospital he was told it would likely take about six months before he could leave the hospital. He denied it, saying he would be home by his daughter's birthday. It was fifteen days away, and he made it! Psalm 91:2 *I will say of the LORD, He is my refuge and my fortress: my God; in him will I trust.*

The doctor expected Ollie to get aspiration pneumonia from breathing in while on fire, but he never got it. He was also prepared to graft skin, but God grew all new skin without the need for any grafts, and he had not one scar on his entire body!

Ollie had many other scrapes with death, but Romans 8:37 says, *Nay, in all these things we are more than conquerors through him that loved us.* He had a heart valve that was nearly non-functioning, and some veins and arteries 95% closed up. When the doctor opened him up and replaced the valve with a pig valve, he found two of the blocked vessels had already built up back-up pathways to supply his heart, so he only had two vessels replaced. The doctor said he heals faster than a teenager.

His entire family sat around the campfire while he told his story and verified it was true. His wife passed away only four months before he shared his testimony, but he is still strong in his faith, spreading the gospel every way he can. I am proud to call Ollie my friend.

Miracle Landing

Our motorcycle buddy told me this amazing testimony. "King Solomon said there is a time to be born and a time to die. It wasn't our time to wake up in heaven. God had mercy on us that beautiful day."

My wife and our small daughter decided it would be a nice day for a plane ride. Our child falls asleep the minute she gets on a plane, so she was dozing. We flew up a few thousand feet and relaxed. With no warning, there was a sudden explosion outside the small cabin. My eyes caught sight of what appeared to be the engine cowling flying above my head over the plane!

The same instant, clear sky appeared in front of me. The propeller was gone! It made no sense. My mind started whizzing through the possibilities. The engine had to be there somewhere or we would have gone into an instant tailspin. Before I could even declare our emergency on the radio, we had dropped to 2500 feet from the ground, falling at the speed of 500 feet a minute.

We were seven miles from an airport and flying over a lake. While my wife prayed fervently for a miracle, I decided to turn around to get off the lake and head for a pasture nearby. The radio contact asked how many were on board, and we proceeded with a crash procedure. Everyone in the control tower was listening as my wife prayed.

The pasture was far too small, surrounded by woods and the lake. I turned off the fuel line. The plane was violently vibrating and falling fast. There would be only one chance of landing and it appeared there was no possibility that we wouldn't crash and burn. Dead ahead of me were two posts with a fence between them. I figured the fence could slow us down. The cows were on their own.

We touched the ground going a hundred miles an hour! It was the roughest plane ride I ever had! Thank God for seatbelts. As we got closer to the fence, I could see the fence posts were actually telephone poles. They were not about to fold on impact. The wings hit those poles at 70 miles an hour, clipping half of one and wiping the other wing off completely, spewing fuel high into the air. That took care of the fire danger.

The engine, held by one bolt, finally broke free and crashed to the ground, causing us to wobble side to side through the pasture. The plane finally took a nosedive into the dirt as the tail flew straight up in the air.

Farmers in vehicles were already in the pasture, having watched the whole miraculous event. Badly shaken, but completely unhurt, we were able to climb out of the wreckage with nothing more than seatbelt marks and tears of joy, in shock at being alive! I believe this was the most amazing moment of my life, and I really don't want any more like that!

Why did the engine explode? I don't have the answer for that one yet. Why did the engine hang on by only one bolt? I would say it had a lot of help from God's guardian angels, guiding us to exactly the right spot, because it was simply not yet our time to die.

Psalm 34:7-8 *The angel of the LORD encampeth round about them that fear him, and delivereth them. ⁸ O taste and see that the LORD is good: blessed is the man that trusteth in him.*

Discussion:
Quote some scriptures that promise God will take care of us.
Are angels able to protect people in emergencies?
Have you ever been rescued by an angel?
If they had not been praying, do you think the end result would have been different?
What does the Bible say about prayer? Angels?

Come Here, Boy

An evangelist friend of ours was preaching at a church, and told us what happened. A boy on the way to that church always walked past the house of a man who was often drunk, and called out nasty remarks to the boy about going to church. One day the man asked the boy why he was going to church.

He said, "People are getting their teeth filled when the evangelist prays for them! I need a filling!" The drunken man thought that was quite hilarious and mocked him unmercifully for his crazy beliefs.

The boy got prayer, and sure enough, God filled his bad tooth, but He only filled it halfway. He was puzzled about it, but left church and headed home.

The drunken fellow was waiting to see what happened, so he called the boy onto his porch and ordered him to open his mouth.

When he opened his mouth, the man examined the filling, and while he watched, God filled the tooth to the top! He sobered up quickly, ran to the church and accepted Jesus!

I have been in such meetings. I read all the controversy about them. Recently I asked Jesus to show me the truth about it. What happened was not that I opened the Book and a verse leaped out at me. God brought me back to every supernatural event in my life, and reminded me He can do anything. I have no time to record all God has done for me. For that reason, when I hear of teeth being filled or straightened or replaced, I know God can do it all, and out of love, He meets all our needs through Christ and His riches in glory. I have no problem with that.

1 Corinthians 2:9 *But as it is written, Eye hath not seen, nor ear heard, neither have entered into the heart of man, the things which God hath prepared for them that love him.*

Two Turn Away Ten Thousand
Pastor Jeanette

I remember 1981 like it was yesterday. We were watching the horse races on TV, having come from Louisville, Kentucky, where everyone is involved in the sport. That was the day I found the lump. Now the word 'lump' doesn't mean much in any circle unless it is found in a person's body. Then it is horrifying!

I avoid medical checkups because God keeps me so healthy I don't need any other doctor, but that lump jerked me to attention with such a start I decided I better get it checked out. Fred went with me, partly to keep me awake after a terrible night with no sleep.

The doctor said she had to do a biopsy right away, even though I insisted it was not necessary.

She told us to relax (yeah, right) in the waiting room and she would call us in after she made the diagnosis.

This woman had the nerve to make me an appointment for surgery the very next Monday at 8 A.M.! "What? Why must you do that? Are you sure it is that important?"

"Absolutely, ma'am. I have seen cancerous tumors just like this take a person's life in only four months. Every day is crucial."

Fred interrupted, saying, "Please don't speak such things into existence to my wife. Jesus is our healer."

You never saw anybody call so many people to pray in all your born days! This was nothing like praying for someone else to be healed. This was me! Sunday I had the whole church lay their hands on my head anointing me with oil, just like James, Jesus' half-brother, told the church we must do to be healed.

The battle in my mind was fierce. I could see myself lying in that casket in four months, my life squelched by the devil in no time at all. I wanted to feel certain nothing would be found and all the prayers would be answered, but my feelings were rampantly out of control!

By Monday morning, I was some kind of weary. The nurse told me to sign the permission papers to do a mastectomy depending on what they found. I flatly refused. Fred promised me they would not take any of my body parts from me. I was so thankful he was with me.

A transport person came with a stretcher to take me to surgery, dressed in my too-short nightie and a funny hat. When we got to the operating room, a nurse got ready to jam an IV needle in the back of my hand and I jerked it back. "Don't you put that in my hand!" I am a pianist, and I was not taking any chances. She inserted it into my forearm instead.

She asked if I wanted to go to sleep. "Oh, please, yes! Anything to stop this incessant worry!"

I groggily woke up to see a face leaning over me. The doctor said she had never seen such a thing! She said, "God gave you a miracle, Jeanette! That tumor was definitely cancer. There was no mistake. I know cancer when I see it. Your tumor was benign, and you are in no danger. You are going to be just fine. I am delighted to give you such good news!"

I do believe I have never been happier about anything in my entire life. I felt so special, so loved, and so grateful that God answered all our prayers for me.

Chapter Two
Angelic Encounters

The Dead Guy

Amazing stories abound. Some are true, and others figments of the imagination, but they are certainly fascinating. The following I believe to be true, told by people I trust, one being me!

A man in our Christian motorcycle group tells of a pickup truck that ran a stop sign, flying right across his path with no way to miss it. His bike was demolished in the crash, but he was transported miraculously over the truck, and landed on the other side on his feet, with his baseball cap still on his head! A policeman came along and asked where the body had been thrown. The biker said, "I'm over here!"

"No," said the policeman, writing up the accident. "I mean the dead guy that was on the motorcycle." He was astounded to discover the cyclist had not been killed or even injured. Both vehicles were going in excess of sixty. Angels are recorded to have appeared to people in the Bible 104 times. There can be no other explanation than angelic assistance. Have you ever seen an angel?

My husband Rog came home from New York City and said he witnessed, outside the Dumont

Hotel, a man in a BMW car whose muffler fell to the ground. A man standing nearby offered to tie it up for a fee. The owner jacked up the car and the man began working on the muffler. The owner went inside a building, and the jack fell, pinning the man underneath! In an instant, while my husband ran over to help, a motorcyclist (an average sized man) stopped his bike, left it running, and picked up the entire back of the thirty-seven hundred pound car! The man was pulled out unhurt! The muscleman got back on his bike and took off, with all the spectators staring at him. Was he an angel? Perhaps.

    The Lord said we would entertain angels unaware. This theory about adrenalin giving supernatural strength is pure speculation and has never been proven. An angel is far more likely to have been there.

    An elder at our church, James Flynn, fell off a porch and broke his wrist. He was about to be discharged from the hospital when he suddenly started hemorrhaging. His spleen burst and to everyone's shock, he passed away.

    What happened next has no explanation. James died about one (?) in the morning, and appeared in a friend's house! Dixie called his wife Gloria the next day and asked her if James had died. "How did you know? Gloria asked her.

"David had gone to bed," Dixie explained, "and I went into a room alone to pray. James Flynn came ***through a wall,*** laughing and happy and looking ten years younger! I asked what he was doing there, and he remarked, 'I'm just passing through, Sis. I've got to go now!' He smiled and left the way he came!"

When Gloria asked her what time this occurred, she was astounded to find it was the same hour James had passed away. Maybe it is our evidence that we will never die, just like Jesus said, but we will all be changed.

We are never to instigate true angelic encounters. People do not conjure up angels or command them to appear. People pray to God in Christ's name and not to the angels. Born-again Christians obey the Word of God in faith.

The devil comes as an angel of light to deceive us. If we 'send' our guardian angel to retrieve our lost items are we stepping into deception? Do we have a right to command angels? What happened in the Bible? This is our guide.

We can ask the Lord to find lost items and He can send an angel, but not us. Nowhere in the Word are people ordering angels around. Put God first, and these things will be added unto you. What things? Whatever we need.

We must never worship angels. We are taught to submit to one another in love and test all things so none of us will be deceived. Knowing the word of God will protect us as we trust those things that line up with the Word alone.

Psalm 34:7 *The angel of the LORD encampeth round about them that fear him, and delivereth them.*

> *Every story has something we can use in our own lives. God's grace is sufficient. Never give up hope. We have free will and our will affects a lot of people-not just us, so we must be careful how we choose. What else did this lesson show you?*

A Light in the Darkness

My husband and I have three sons, and they all love danger. As a result, we have many stories to share! This is a brief excerpt of one adventure.

Dave, Tom, and Rob packed up their diving gear a few years ago and headed to the Florida springs, known for amazing limestone caves. None of them were certified for cave diving, but an experienced diver invited them to follow his line as he went deeper, ahead of them. He told them to go into the first room, and turn right around. "Don't stay in that cave more than a couple minutes. Many lives have been lost in these caves," he warned them.

They followed the diver's lifeline that led them down a narrow serpentine passageway into the cave one hundred ten feet below the surface. Being amateurs, they didn't know the minimum supplies for the basic cave diver were at least three lights, two tanks, two regulators, and special reels of high-grade nylon line to guide the way.

As they entered the large sparkling room with their $5 glued-together flashlights, Tom and Rob floated upward. Dave instinctively dropped the lifeline and followed their lights. He could barely see their outline at the very top when his light flickered off. Trouble was brewing. His heart sank.

He settled to the floor, and found the line had disappeared below two feet of thick silt. Fear crept in further as Tom's light flickered and went out. All three frantically sought the exit, but couldn't find it. Only Rob's light remained. Tanks crashed against the walls as they swam into crevices to find the tunnel.

They used up precious air seeking a way of escape. It had taken a half hour to get into the cave; Dave's air was nearly gone. He knew for certain his time had come to meet God, and realized his wife and two young daughters would be devastated. He sank to the bottom in despair. All light left as Rob and Tom tried to gouge their way through the rock ceiling. As Dave sat alone in the dark, a thought came to him. *God, please help me find the lifeline.*

The line was suddenly in his hand! He had lost it beneath two feet of silt with no hope of finding it but there it was! *God*, he prayed silently. *Now I don't know which way to go!*

A voice spoke clearly to him. "Follow the current. It was against you going in." He was shocked to get an answer, and even more amazed as his light flashed on for his brothers, frozen in fear above him.

They swam out much quicker as the current sucked them out and upward. Dave had the least air but they all had to take time to decompress before shooting to the top. When they surfaced, all three came up screaming, "Thank you, God!"

The next week, tragically, three other brothers lost their lives in those caves. The strangest thing about that was my new neighbor read my story and said, "You won't believe this, but I came from Iowa and those three boys used to eat at my table. They played with my children years ago."

When we get to heaven, we will understand the real details of this adventure. (The complete story is published in *"The Desk in the Attic."* at Booklockerbooks.com)

John 10:27 (KJV) *My sheep hear my voice, and I know them, and they follow me.*

Chapter Three
Deliverance and Cults

We are More Than Conquerors
By Marilyn

I have a sad story to tell of my past, but do not cry for me as I'm no longer in that pit. Jesus pulled me out of that pit, that miry clay and sat me on higher ground, on the Rock. It's only by His grace and His mercy in my life that I am here to write this story and I write it to glorify Him. As what he has done for me, He can also do for you.

My alcoholic father sexually molested me with incest between the ages of five and seven, and there were other sexual abuses after that by babysitters, and friends of the family and such. My childhood was very unstable. My mom remarried when I was seven and we moved - and moved and moved. You probably won't be surprised to know I married and divorced two abusive men with alcohol and drug problems. I wasn't able to have children due to the severe sexual abuse of my childhood.

After my second divorce I tried to commit suicide. I was so full of pain; blocked memories of my sexual abuses flooded my mind. There was so much anger and bitterness, total lack of trust, especially regarding men. I felt so much rejection all my life. I was a people pleaser and unable to say no. I had so much shame and unforgiveness, guilt and low self-esteem. I felt ugly and lonesome and betrayed even though I was a spirit-filled Christian that went to church regularly.

So I decided to end it all. I couldn't take any more! I had to get out. I drank a lot of hard liquor and took a whole handful of pain pills, Percocet and Darvocet. God was apparently not ready to give up on me, even though I sure was. I fell asleep and didn't wake up for fifteen hours! I was not a happy camper when I woke without a hangover or even a headache! I was so angry and disappointed.

This was my turning point. God started me on my journey of healing. One of the first books I read after my suicide attempt was "Root of Rejection" by Joyce Meyers. I wept through every word of it and

I highly recommend it. I also got a revelation of God's agape unconditional love, no comparison to the perverted love I was raised with.

As I walk the journey out of pain I receive more healing each step I take. I'm walking out of the pain of my past and into 'joy unspeakable and full of glory!' I'm walking out of self-hatred and anger and bitterness and into His mercy and grace. I'm walking out of rejection and shame and guilt into His great love and peace.

He has and is delivering me of all the ugliness of my childhood. Where I had unforgiveness there is now much forgiveness. He has restored me and I have many reasons to celebrate. Also He's given me a godly husband that I'm learning to trust and respect. God is so awesome and what He has done for me He will do for you as well.

The Bible says in Psalm 139:14: "I am fearfully and wonderfully made; marvelous are thy works."

I just want to tell you that you are valuable. You are significant, and He loves you unconditionally.

Another thing I want to talk about is accountability. Yes, awful things happened to me at the hands of others and it wasn't my fault that these things happened, BUT it's my pain and my anger and my rejection and I can't blame others any more. I'm accountable for all these things and I've given them to the Lord and asked Him-of my own free will-to help undo the damage of my past. He has never disappointed me.

It's my miracle that I'm alive today and can tell you about God's goodness in my life and I give Him all the glory.

> *This story is filled with supernatural interventions from God. What Satan meant for evil, God turned out for good. He protected Marilyn from dying when she had not even asked, and had done all she could to leave this pain-filled world behind. God had a plan that did not include suicide.*
>
> *How can God heal a heart filled with bitterness, distrust and pain? He destroyed the lies she believed about herself and others. When she decided to believe God, He softened her heart and showed her nothing can keep her from His love. She learned the power in forgiveness, and looks forward to eternity without any more pain-ever.*

Marilyn Shares Miracles

I wanted one of those little digital clocks that stick on a mirror, so I started shopping. For a year, I never ran across one. Then one day a friend in another state I rarely heard from sent me a letter and in the envelope was-guess what? A tiny digital clock! Does God know our hearts? Oh, yes, He knows us better than we know ourselves!

My sister and her husband were hooked on drugs a long time. I prayed for them and worried about their salvation a lot once I got saved, but it seemed my prayers were not reaching heaven. But lo and behold, one day they found themselves in a Pentecostal church and a spiritual magnet drew them to the front altar for prayer.

The pastor must have had a pretty close walk with God because they both suddenly fell to the floor like dead people! They went under God's spiritual knife and He did surgery on their hearts. When they got up, the need and desire for drugs was gone! They never went through any withdrawal. It was over!

I damaged my lower back years ago. The pain was almost unbearable. I couldn't even get off the couch unless I rolled on my knees to the floor to get up and walk. I felt impressed by the Holy Spirit for some reason I still cannot explain to anoint my doors and windows with oil. Oil in the Bible is a symbol of the Holy Spirit. God told elders in the Bible to anoint the sick with oil and the prayer of faith would heal the sick. In the Old Testament, God separated people for special tasks by sending a prophet to anoint them or pour oil on their heads as a sign of God's call on their lives. It can be any kind of oil, but olive oil seems to be what was used then.

Over the period of just one day, I gradually noticed my back kept improving until that same day the pain totally disappeared! Who is this God that we serve? The Holy Spirit teaches us in the most amazing ways.

> *Just do what God tells us, and leave the rest up to Him. "Be anxious for nothing, but in prayer and supplication with thanksgiving, make your requests known to God."*

Marilyn Kiser has written a wonderful book on deliverance from the pain of incest and abuse. It is available on amazon.com, called "The Need for Healing...Continues, My Journey out of Pain.

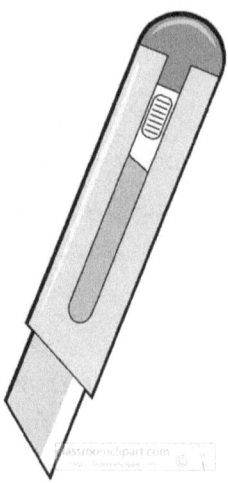

Why Do We Hurt Ourselves?

This young woman told me how she was set free. We will call her Janice.

"How far down must a person fall before he sees the truth? I fell nearly into hell before I was rescued. I spent thirteen years of my life where I was merely escaping the inevitable, thirteen years without God.

I was left with a crying mother and a heart full of unbearable demons. Who would have known God could pour such great miracles into such a life, while every day I lived in fear, believing forgiveness and acceptance was impossible. One question tormented me. Why was it so easy to believe in the devil, yet so hard to believe in God?

I remember growing up as a kid; my grandma was very religious and I attended her church with my friends. I was never forced to go. I didn't really understand much of it, but I always had fun. Then I became a teenager.

There is always that one crowd that doesn't make right choices. I was one of those people who felt like they really didn't fit in. I saw the kids around me in school as sociable, easily liked, and I would even say normal or average. I had no idea it was normal to feel like a misfit as a teenager. We will avoid the pain of rejection at all cost. We want to fit in, but we don't know what extremes are required from that particular group and at what point we need to stop or bail out. I just wanted to belong.

Not yet mature enough to make wise choices, I ended up choosing the wrong friends. As a result I did a lot of things I regret. It is said that you become like those you hang out with; birds of a feather flock together; and my choice of friends forever changed my life.

Exposure to what they liked changed my taste in music to hardcore rock with screaming and rage, which influenced a change in my appearance. I started to dress with all black clothing and tricked-out hair. I started to drift into the 'Satanist' stuff, because somewhere in my mind it made sense, but it sucked me down a path toward death. First came depression, then self-mutilation and finally thoughts of suicide. My life spiraled downward and soon I just wanted my life to end. I lost the nice friends I did have, confused my family, and even more important, I lost a part of myself.

Mutilating one's self has confused the experts for ages. It used to be considered a failed suicide attempt, but that is not it. People with addictions are similar in the sense they have somehow lost control of what they do to themselves. Some other power takes them over. It is the same once a person starts cutting himself. It seems to give a feeling of relief, even though it is shocking to feel the pain and see your blood pour out of your body. What does a person gain by such an action? It was simply a step into the occult world brought about by crazy music and irrational thought patterns where there were no boundaries.

I can remember every detail of the day I first tried it. With a rusty old carpenter knife, I slit my arm open, and by the time I was done, I had more than sixty cuts scattered all along my body. I remember the look on my mom's face! She walked into my room and found me holding a bloody towel with a knife to my wrist. I knew what I was doing was destructive and wrong and didn't understand what made me even do such a thing. I wanted to die of shame. I felt like the most worthless person and a huge disappointment to my family. Suicide seemed like my only option. If I could have sunk through the floor, I would have.

This awful obsession continued in secret, and made me very weak, emotionally, mentally, and physically. One day I simply fell apart, crying and trembling, too weak even to walk. My mom was exhausted, having tried everything she knew, at her wits' end, with no idea how to stop me from self-destruction.

I made the choice to admit myself into a hospital with some hope that I'd get well. I remember my mom bringing me a Bible. With not much else to do there, terribly confused and hopeless, I decided to read my new Bible and pray. I was eventually released from the hospital and had gained a bit of faith and hope, but not enough to solve my problems, still struggling with depression.

During this process of change, my mom introduced me to her friend Stella, who took me to church with her, but the problem continued; I was still not free, and my faith in God was still zero to none. The pastor's words made no sense and the thought of God's love and forgiveness was just a lie to me.

Stella became a guardian to me, like the light at the end of a tunnel. She kept bringing me to her church where I met A LOT of really nice people. I didn't really believe anything the pastor preached. I was just stubborn and didn't want to accept the facts about Jesus, and that someone actually cared.

Once again, I was admitted into another hospital, but this time I was starting to gain a new perspective. I remember how everyone there thought I was crazy because I would sit there by myself in a corner, look up at the sky and just cry and scream to God. In my room I would sing and pray to him on my knees just asking, "Why?" I finally just surrendered. I got on my knees in my room and said, "God, I have no direction other than you to help me through this all. I just need your hand in guidance to lead my way." This time I kept my head focused on getting better. I prayed desperate prayers every single night I was there.

That day, I could tell everything in me had changed. I was discharged from the hospital with a completely new perspective and with God as my Lord and Savior. I went to my church and confessed my faith in Jesus Christ and was saved. I realized Jesus paid for my sins and wrong ways. I feel accepted and not so alone. I started to see my life turn around as God began having his way with me.

Today, I see everything different. I no longer turn to cutting to solve my problems. My music has turned to worship and my clothes are full of color. God is now the one I turn to whenever any problem arises. He continues to make changes in my life every day and is guiding me on my path to change the world around me. That decision to be saved was the best one I could ever make because only God can turn lives into miracles. I will never forget what he has done for me. I've been attending church and I try to help them out whenever I can. They showed me Jesus and gave me hope. I am ready for whatever life has in store for me, and I feel like I can take on the world. "Life is meant to be lived in one direction-upward." God CHANGED my life.

The hospital contained me and protected me for a time, but only God set me free, using Psalm 6:1-10.

The Grail Movement

Ed went to our church for a while. This is his story.

"I have many testimonies to give in praise to my Lord and Savior Jesus Christ who has done lots of amazing things in my life, and this is my first one. I'm now surrendered to Him completely as He begins to work through me for His glory.

My parents were Methodists and I grew up with the Methodist hymns and songs and was enrolled in the local Methodist church choir in James Town, Ghana, West Africa.

I did not like going to church because I had no clothes or shoes, but my late father did not care.

He forced us to go to church. My dad was a strict disciplinarian and he taught us how to obey or be disciplined, so I went to church grudgingly. As soon as I was able to earn my own living, I became independent and stopped going to church.

I met a Greek businessman who introduced me to big business, and the more money I made, the farther became my distance from the Lord. I did not pray and did not have a Bible, though I had a collection of books and magazines, including Playboy. I was in the entertainment business and thought having fun was all there was to life. I had an acute sense of making money. I thought it was all my idea or ingenuity and never gave any credit or glory to God.

When business began to fail, I found myself running from place to place, seeking help. During this time I came across many spiritualists, occultists, and the traditional African jujumen.

They worked magic, and had all kinds of charms, talismans, spells and potions. I consulted these people for guidance, protection and success, not knowing this was an abomination to the Lord.

I have since repented and no longer have any business with such unfruitful works of darkness. I learned these people have no real power. That power belongs to the Lord alone, but this realization came much later, after I had been though a lot of storms.

In my quest for success, I became a member of the Grail Movement, an organization that claimed to believe in Jesus, but whose doctrines were unscriptural. I did not realize this until ten years later when I finally left. The Grail Movement originated in Germany in the late 1940s. Worldwide, there are about 10,000 members.

This turn of events came when I met a man of God, who introduced me to Jesus Christ. I heard the gospel for the first time in my life, and realized that the Bible is the only true and living Word of God. There are many books in the world, but the Bible is Spirit and Life, and is the revelation of God Himself to man. There is no knowledge or understanding of God anywhere but through His own Word, which He reveals to us in the Bible.

I have been a born-again believer since 1994 and have been trying to share the Word of God with others. One thing I know; *Jesus is the only way to salvation, for there is no other name under heaven given among men whereby we must be saved.* Acts 4:12. *Jesus is the way, the Truth, and the Life, and no one comes to God but by Him alone.* John 14:6. The idea that there are many ways to God is a doctrine of demons and must be rejected by all who want salvation.

The Bread of Life

Mark is another friend who shared his testimony at dinner one evening.

"I was raised in the Catholic Church. I followed all the rules and did what I was told, but when I got to college I found other ways to live. I had no limitations, so I did whatever felt good, like drinking. I met my future wife and eventually we were married.

My wife gave birth to two sons. One is now in the army overseas and the other, I am not sure where he is. Our marriage seemed to be all right. My wife was a take-control kind of person, and I resented that, so we argued a lot.

One day after several years of marriage, my wife announced she was throwing in the towel and getting a divorce. I was blown away. I had no idea it had gone so far. I was beside myself. The pain of rejection was almost unbearable. Even alcohol didn't numb the sting of it. Panic attacks began hitting me. Finances became a bigger struggle than ever. I had no idea where to turn. My life was falling apart.

We continued to live in the same house because she couldn't afford a divorce, but it was not pleasant. Someone suggested a counselor might help. The company I worked for paid for it, so we went. It was about a hundred dollars an hour, but it didn't work, either. We used it to get even, and accuse each other of things. We left every time fighting. The counselor finally asked me if I went to church. I badmouthed religion, saying it was a farce.

The next week, however, I decided in desperation to try it just one more time. I went down to St. Jude's in Sandy Springs near my home. I did my best to listen and glean whatever I could, but I left empty, determined not to return.

I did return, however, and once again worked hard to catch something hopeful for my life. I got a tiny bit of helpful information. One day I was invited to a Cursillo. The guy from church said a bunch of men hang together and do some Bible studies, eat great meals, and fellowship for three days, get away from it all - and it was free. I don't know what made me do it, but I agreed to go. Well, that was the turning point.

Only those that have been to one of these can understand what it is about. You can't put it into words. It was structured to help you find your way through life, and I sure needed that. It met my need in astounding ways. The last day they were having communion and I had decided I was not going to take it, now that I understood what it meant and the consequences of taking it unworthily.

The Matzoth bread was passed. Suddenly, I knew I had to take it, and I grabbed a piece and stuffed it into my mouth. I believe that was the moment of decision. I had accepted Jesus into my heart that very minute, and I knew who He was. God opened my eyes as I responded to His invitation, and I became a born-again person, brand new on the inside, with God's spirit having entered me. I don't mean this in a physical sense, that I literally ate Jesus' body. It was a transformation because I surrendered to Him, and He in turn revealed Himself to me. I was thirty-three, the same age of Jesus when He was killed.

On the way home, 'my head' told me, "Go home and love your wife. Love never fails." What? Why do I have to change? It came to me again. When I walked in the door, my wife shot both barrels at me, haranguing and baiting me for a fight. I said, "I had a good weekend and I am not going to ruin it. I am going to bed."

Over time, as the change in my heart grew, I started taking the boys to church. I bought a new Bible and read it early every morning. God began teaching me how to live and how to love.

A Methodist church near our house had some activities for the kids and we got to know the folks there a bit. Pat said one day, "You know, I have seen a big change in you. How about I go with you and we visit that church?" I was willing to try anything by then.

One Sunday we left church after the pastor had preached about being saved, and Pat quietly said, "I did it."

"You did what?"

"I invited Jesus into my heart."

Our life took a huge turnaround that day. That simple act of sensing Jesus was knocking on the door of her heart, and her response added a sixth dimension to her life. God came in- Father, Son, and Holy Spirit got involved with my wife.

We lived together in relative harmony for the next twenty-four years. Seven years ago, my wife went to Peru on a mission trip and preached to the women there with a great response, with many souls saved. She became a wonderful teacher of the Word of God, until she died of cancer six years ago.

Since then, I have remarried a wonderful woman named Patti who loves evangelism like I do. We spend part of nearly every day sharing the gospel one place or another. Life can't be better!

Women's Aglow

A friend shared her testimony with me at a motorcycle rally.

"A friend invited me one day to a Christian meeting called, "Women's Aglow." I had never heard of it, but told her I would be busy playing tennis the next day and couldn't come. That night, the stars were brightly shining that night, so I assumed I would be playing tennis. Suddenly in the middle of the night, a violent storm began, lasting into the morning.

"I guess I will be going to Women's Aglow," I said to myself. I got up early to make donuts at the restaurant, and went with my friend to the meeting.

A harpist was playing the most gorgeous music when we walked in and sat down. It was so powerful, I started weeping with emotion! Then the speaker started giving her testimony about God. I didn't understand all of it, but at the end she said, "If there is more, don't you want to know what it is?"

I was raised a Christian Scientist since childhood, and never considered there was anything more than I had or believed in. I was satisfied that I got it all. But that statement kept ringing in my ears. "If there is more, would you like to have it?"

By the time she had repeated it through her talk at least six times, I finally decided to go up and ask her, "What more is there? Tell me what I have to do to get it." She led me to pray the "Sinner's prayer", a prayer admitting I was a sinner and was asking Jesus to forgive me and come into my heart. Well, I had always been taught that we were not sinners.

Suddenly in the midst of my reasoning, the Holy Spirit reminded me of something I had done that this woman would have called a sin. So I was free to pray the prayer. As a result, my life changed so much that my husband soon realized I had something he wanted, so he prayed with me and got saved too. I am so grateful to God for finding us both.

Chapter Four
Finding Jesus

A Gift of Miracles

It all began in 1973 when Jesus Christ burst into my life. Here I was, 32 years old, teaching Sunday school, and I didn't even know Jesus personally. He knew I had been looking for Him but in all the wrong places.

The pastor must have figured it out, so he set up meetings for all teachers every night for a week. One evening we went around the circle and simply said, "Jesus is Lord." I got tongue-tied! I could not say those words! I finally blurted them out and ran out the door weeping.

That Sunday James Kennedy spoke on a tape in church and challenged us to imagine Jesus grabbing our hand as we raised it as an act of faith. I did, and in a spiritual way, Jesus revealed Himself to me at that moment! I knew that I knew Jesus was real. Amazing. I was so shocked to find He was alive, I found myself in elevators and on sidewalks coming up to strangers, saying, "Do you know that Jesus is still alive?"

A few asked me some questions, and wanted to meet Him. I had a chance to tell them the good news that Jesus paid for all their sins on the cross. All they had to do was believe on Him. Several strangers were interested enough to stop, right on the street, pray with me to know Jesus, and leave with their prayer answered. The Bible says it is the Holy Spirit who reveals who Jesus is. God was kind enough to put prepared people across my path to encourage me to keep sharing about Him.

From the moment He came into my life, I started seeing miracles. I have shared some in detail and will share more soon. After I became a Christian, I started tithing ten percent of my grocery money, and that year my (then unbelieving) husband's salary doubled!

We had a hailstorm and prayed God would protect our garden, and the hailstones surrounded the garden without touching one plant! All the neighbors' gardens were destroyed. I didn't yet know enough to pray for them, too.

My husband lost vision in his eye from diabetic retinopathy, received prayer and anointing with oil for healing, and the next day God healed 39 blood vessels in his eye that had broken. The doctor was amazed.

Thirteen members of my immediate family received Jesus as Savior within a year after I stuffed a written prayer for them in a crack of the Wailing Wall in Jerusalem. Superstition? I thought so until I looked back and remembered that prayer.

A month after I was saved, I bought my husband two suits at a great sale for $40 each. When I got home, I found they had only charged me ten dollars each! I was tempted to not mention it (my old ways coming out) but God showed me it was important to be honest. I called the store, and the manager told me to keep them and was shocked I had called. I learned a big lesson. God knows everything we do, and uses things that happen as lessons.

I loved garage sales, and found from experience that I could ask God to help me find items my family needed, so I always made a list and prayed over it. My friend refused to believe God would do such things, so she went with me. It was such fun to see her face every time I found something on the list. I needed a door for our cottage. I asked Him for a solid wood door with a window in it for some reason. I passed a pile of trash on a curb, and there was an oak door on the stack-

with a square window in it! I quickly got out of the car and measured it and it was exactly the right size. I knocked on the door and asked if I could have it. The lady was delighted to give it to me. Each item I found was miraculous.

We were finally ready to head home with everything from the list in the car except one thing. My grandson is musically inclined, and I wanted to give him a keyboard. She started giving me a hard time about not having found it. Suddenly we passed a sign for a sale, so I turned around to check it out. Sure enough! There was a beautiful brand new keyboard, no less, and the price was only $20. It even had a full set of D batteries and ran perfectly! That was not a need but just something he wanted. She never went with me again.

A third of the ministry Jesus did on earth involved His miracles. He said we that believe would do the same things He did on earth, and we would do even greater things because He was going to heaven, sending His Holy Spirit down to give us power.

One of the gifts of the spirit is a gift of miracles, so maybe that is why I see so many. Faith also comes as we study His words and conquer the doubts so deeply instilled in us. It seems to grow stronger after we actually experience one, of course. Then comes another! On a roll!

Sometimes the miracle is so profound that God has to drop a special gift of faith into us. Out of the heart the mouth speaks. Life and death is in the power of the tongue, so faith often involves more than simply believing. It is important that we confess what we believe, and thank Him even before we receive it. Nothing is impossible with God. You can study gifts of the spirit in 1 Cor.12-14.

This Little Light of Mine

Alicia is a remarkable lady who learned the truth about Jesus as a teenager in Mexico. Eventually she and her pastor husband took in forty orphans in Mexico.

Persecution broke out against the orphanage and the children have all been taken away and placed in government care in Mexico. Alicia has been sought and her life threatened. She has found refuge in America.

She had no funds, but God sent someone to give her a tiny trailer and a small piece of land. There was no water or electricity in the trailer, but she made the best of it.

The trailer was in an area of drug addicts, filth, sin, regular shootings, and there was trash everywhere! Even the police would not come near. She became depressed and cried out to God, "Lord, What have I done for you to chasten me this way?"

He answered her, saying that He came down from a Holy place to a similar 'trash dump' two thousand years ago and stayed for thirty-three years. He said, "You have never said "no" to Me. I love you." She wept with relief.

Alicia asked God to remove the horrible stench of garbage everywhere. One day, a garbage truck drove into the neighborhood, stopped in front of her house and said they had orders to come there! They never came there, they said. She began praising God, and learned the driver was a Christian! For *three weeks* they hauled garbage. She never knew who hired them.

Alicia's daughter eventually came to stay with her. They worked on the tiny yard every day, and gradually the neighbors followed suit! A seed of respectability was blooming.

The downcast group of neighbors rarely even lifted their heads to look at her, but Alicia always spread her smile and love upon them anyhow, saying, "God loves you." She never told anyone she was a well-known evangelist, but one night a pickup truck roared right onto her lawn and the distraught driver slammed on the brakes just before running into her trailer. She ran out, and the driver sat in the seat weeping loudly! He said, "I want to kill my neighbor!" The Holy Spirit led him to her door.

Alicia prayed quickly, "What do I say, Lord?" Then she said to the man, "Did you give this man his life? Why would you want to kill him? Change your mind, right now, and pray with me. You want change?"

"Yes!" he cried. "Jesus, come into my heart!"

Alicia told him to confess, 'I am free!' He did. She immediately brought him over to tell the man he forgave him, and to his amazement, his neighbor and entire family accepted Jesus! They have all been baptized in water and in the Holy Spirit. This was a major breakthrough. God has since called this man who wanted to murder, to become a pastor!

After a year in her "little cave" as she calls her tiny house, the area is clean and respectable, and she has weekly Bible studies for adults and teachers for the children. She also has organized a prayer meeting in which fifty pastors and wives meet to intercede for America!

They pray for our President's safety and wisdom. She said if we do not pray for our leaders, our country will lose its freedom, like many others have.

One day, a pastor friend called Alicia, and told her he could not bear to be present when his aunt passed away. Alicia said she would go and pray for her. God said to her, "I Am." That's all. When they went to the hospital, there were three beds in one room. A very ill woman with cancer was there, with oxygen mask, and tubes plugged in every orifice, surely dying. The doctor came in and told the pastor she had a few hours left, and that they had to plan for it. Alicia felt it was 'bells from the devil' playing when he said that. She took the woman's hand. "You are healed in Jesus' name."

The pastor's aunt said, "Yes!" The nurse came in, and she told her to take out the tubes! The nurse could not do that, so the woman removed her mask. The next day she was discharged, perfectly healed!

That same evening, Alicia was led to pray for a young girl in the other bed. She had been in an accident, and was declared in a vegetative state. She was unable to do anything, much less talk. Alicia went to her, and asked the family her name. The girl suddenly said, "Anna!" They were all astounded! Then she said, "Mama, I want to go home!" The next day she, too, was discharged, completely healed!

Because Alicia is sold out to God, knows what His word says, studies it diligently every day, and obeys Him, signs and wonders follow her as He promised. She shared one more of many recent miracles. A ninety-four year old man had cancer on his face. He looked shockingly grotesque, with a huge growth on his cheek the size of a melon. Alicia thought she would pray for the Lord to take him to heaven. But she did not know he would not have gone to heaven! God spoke to her and said, "I want to give life. Do not see him in the flesh." She anointed the man with oil, and he yelled, in Spanish, "Bless God!" He was healed and born again!

Alicia explained that the anointing breaks the yoke, according to the Bible. Lazarus was brought back to life. He came out of the tomb, but was still bound. Jesus did not untie him. He said to others, "Loose him!" We are called to do the same. She loosed this man from cancer in Jesus' name.

Alicia has the power God promised to those that will believe and put Him first. There is a form of godliness in the world, but a denial of this kind of power. It comes when nothing matters more than our relationship with God. True humility is a key that opens doors for us. It is the kind of humility that knows we do not save ourselves with our works. It depends only on God to save us and not anything we can do. Oswald Chambers said that the best statement we can make that pleases God is that we are saved, sanctified and going to heaven, because Jesus paid the price!

John 15:4 (KJV) *Abide in me, and I in you. As the branch cannot bear fruit of itself, except it abide in the vine; no more can ye, except ye abide in me.*

The Most Spectacular Miracle

My dear friend and neighbor Bernice was born in 1922. She has trusted Jesus as her Savior since 1935. She often tells me about life when she was young. It is hard to imagine having had no running water in the house, no bathrooms, a woodstove, no refrigeration, and when a car came down the dirt road all the kids in school ran to the windows to see it.

More inventions and discoveries have occurred in the last hundred years than the world ever had in all the years prior to that time, and she has seen most of them. None of these things, however, surpass a human being turning into a new creature! That is what happened to Bernice and everyone else who has ever been confronted with the offer to invite Jesus into his heart.

She attended a little Baptist church, walking a few miles to get there unless a horse and wagon was available. One Sunday morning in her thirteenth year she became terribly uneasy with the sermon and felt a decision of some sort had to be made *that* day. A song tore at her heart. The pastor read the verse, "Behold, I stand at the door and knock," Jesus said. "If anyone will open the door and let Me come in, I will come and commune with him." Rev.3:20

A war was raging inside her heart that she did not comprehend. Satan knew it was God's time for her to know Jesus. "If only someone had taken my hand and led me up to the altar, I know I would have come," Bernice said, "but nobody knew the battle that was raging in me."

Terrible thoughts flooded her mind. "God doesn't love me like He loves my friends. He doesn't want me. What is wrong with me? " Self-pity overwhelmed her that morning, and she ran out of the church nearly in tears over the words in her brain. She seemed unaware that Satan was her enemy and able to plant thoughts in her mind.

She went to a different church the next week hoping the feeling would go away, but she had no peace. The Hound of Heaven was getting her attention, wooing her to Him. John 3:16 said "For God so loved the world, that he gave his only begotten Son, that whosoever believeth in him should not perish, but have everlasting life." She didn't understand He was offering her salvation if she would simply give in to God.

The next Sunday she returned to the little Baptist church, and when the pastor offered to pray with anyone who would come forward to him, Bernice's hands locked onto the chair in front of her. She couldn't get her white-knuckled hands free! Some invisible force was holding them tightly to the chair.

Suddenly she asked God to help her, and she found herself in front of the church with no recollection of how she got there. Weeping with relief, she prayed with the pastor as life's burdens rolled off. Jesus poured His Spirit into her heart to reside there forever. She suddenly felt clean and pure like she was born all over again. God said once we invite Jesus into our lives, we become different. Our spirit is washed with His blood, our sin is erased, and we enter the Kingdom of God.

Bernice Tallant spends her life serving everyone around her. Feeding people is her love language. We will all remember her saying, "Oh, please let me bring you supper!" When she leaves for heaven, we will miss her love, but will see her again for eternity. We will also miss those suppers, fried chicken, cole slaw, green beans, biscuits, mashed potatoes and gravy, her favorites, followed by pecan pie. Yummy.

2 Peter 3:9 *The Lord is not slack concerning his promise, as some men count slackness; but is longsuffering to us-ward, not willing that any should perish, but that all should come to repentance.*

Bernice did pass away of congestive heart failure as this book was being assembled, on March 10, 2015.

Acts 2:21 (KJV) *And it shall come to pass, that whosoever shall call on the name of the Lord shall be saved.*

Examine your Bible as a precious document and see what you have inherited. The treasures awaiting you are mighty. If you only knew what is offered, you would never hoard. It shall be a source of delight to you to see the foolishness of humanity to fear poverty when such riches are in store, available on request mixed with faith. Faith is the assurance of things unseen and the claim of a promise yet unrealized. James said a double-minded man does not receive anything from God, so we must have all doubts settled and gone.

Chapter Five
Dreams and Visions

I Loved Donuts More Than I Loved God

This came to me in the night out of nowhere. "You love donuts more than Me." Is it true? Is it revelation from God? Maybe it is an answer to my question. I had gone to bed, saying, "Lord, search my heart and reveal to me any sin in my life."

I fell asleep. The short chubby Dunkin Donut man was just waking up. He looked outside at the full moon, high overhead, got dressed and drove to work in his little white truck.

I watched in my dream as he entered the bakery at the back of the store. He got right to work, emptying a huge bag of flour and other ingredients into the boggiest bowl I'd ever seen. Before long the dough was kneaded into a fat elastic band. The little baker transferred it to another strange machine and turned it on. Soon it extruded perfect little donuts, ready to grow into my favorite junk food.

Once they had each puffed up twice their original size, he dumped batches of donuts into hot grease where they grew even bigger.

From there they went into a glaze bath, made of sugar, butter and other yummy stuff. He lovingly lifted each shiny gem out of the frosting bath with a spatula and set it on a display tray.

By then my mouth was watering all over the pillow. Before I woke up, I must have devoured at least a dozen.

Then I heard that gentle loving voice again. "You love donuts more than you love Me."

I knew it was my dearest Friend, Jesus, doing His best to jar me back to my senses.

He knew these donuts were an idol to me. If He asked me to do something and someone put in front of me a warm sweet glazed donut, I would instantly dismiss His request and gobble it down. How different is that from a Buddhist, given a choice of bowing to Jesus or a statue?

Donuts are my favorite idol, but like the Hindus who worship hundreds of idols, I have many food favorites I love.

Now that the Lord revealed my sin, what must I do? I can't have two masters. I will love the one and hate the other. If I choose food over obedience to God, I am already turning away from Him, and one day may reject Him completely. Once He shows me the truth, I must make a choice.

My relationship with God is more precious than diamonds or donuts! I want Jesus to rule my life, not my body. What will happen when Satan, God's enemy and mine, sets me up again? I have no power in my flesh to resist them. Something in me gets anxious if I even think of refusing that donut.

Once God pointed out my sin of idolatry, I confessed I had been sinning- for years. I asked Him to forgive me, and I know He did because of I John 1:9. *If we confess our sins, he is faithful and just to forgive us our sins, and to cleanse us from all unrighteousness.*

The first temptation came a week later. The pastor had a birthday, and the elders hired Krispy Kreme bakers to serve every hungry member a fresh wonderful GLAZED DONUT at noon as we left the church. I wasn't even safe in church!

You guessed it. I failed the very first test. How could I do such a thing, after Jesus showed me it was idolatry for me? I realized it would not be an easy transition to put God first. Habits die hard.

Avoiding others who loved donuts more than God was difficult, but I soon found new friends that served Christ alone, and they often prayed for me to overcome. (Some people can eat donuts and for them it is not sin, but they were too important to me, and opened the door for other unhealthy food and vices.)

I found verses to memorize and quote aloud that gave my spirit strength over what my body wanted. Best of all, I grew to love my wonderful Friend Jesus so much, donuts no longer even tempted me.

I Peter 1:13 *Therefore, prepare your minds for action; be self-controlled, set your hope fully on the grace to be given you when Jesus Christ is revealed.*

The Twilight Zone

I was walking to the grocery store that gorgeous spring morning. The birds were chirping, the smell of new flowers was glorious, the neighbors were out trimming and cleaning up after winter, and I felt great!

Something occurred in a moment of time that changed this day so completely; nothing will ever be the same again! It was as though I walked through a mirror, right there on the sidewalk. I didn't notice it, but looking back, this is what it must have been like:

"I glance at my wrinkled hands – the ones with the liver spots multiplying daily, the ones with the swollen arthritic joints, ridged nails from lack of some mineral or another…and suddenly I see hands that are young, beautiful, supple, and smooth. This gets my attention. I notice my sore hip no longer hurts, and walking is effortless, but my vision is terribly blurred! Removing my glasses, I find my ability to see is awesome! I can see blocks away without any trouble. What is going on here?

Something quite profound and unexplainable has given me these new hands and perfect vision! Am I dreaming? That is not possible. Dreams don't show up during a walk.

All right, I say to myself. *Either God just performed an amazing miracle, or I am hallucinating. I must evaluate this and gather some facts.* I keep walking- without glasses. The grass is a magnificent green, the breathtaking flowers all perfect – and I notice the absence of anything dead! There are no dead branches; no wilting plants, and no piles of old leaves anywhere!

The sidewalk has an appearance of a material like.... gold! It is a soft shade of pale yellow patina, not slippery, easy to glide on, and embossed, like a leather pattern.

Ahead of me are things so glorious there are no words to describe them. I see objects beyond the scope of my wildest imagination.

Suddenly I hear music – or sounds that almost lift me into the air! Ecstatic new emotions pulsate through every cell of my being! I want to stay here forever! But I must find out where I am and how I arrived.

A gentle breeze begins to caress me. I look at my feet, and they are no longer on the sidewalk!

I am floating easily a few feet above the ground. I'm not afraid, but astounded! I lift my arms and rise even higher! Soon I'm above the treetops having a glorious experience!

Ahead of me I see a beautiful high wall, brilliantly sparkling. Every color bounces in moving effervescent rainbows against the wall and out again. The wall appears to be alive from the motion of the rainbows.

A high luminescent pearl gate, like a vast bracelet clasp, begins to open. I slowly lower my arms and glide downward, descending toward the gate. A majestic tall man offers me his hand. I reach to him, and he gently takes my hand and leads me through the gate.

Suddenly, everything turns pitch black, I feel very dizzy and confused. Echoes fill my entire brain. The dentist is urgently calling my name, telling me to wake up. "It is time to go home."

"No!! This is not real! I am not going!"

One of these days, it will be no longer a dream, but reality.

Rev. 21:1-3 *Now I saw a new heaven and a new earth, for the first heaven and the first earth had passed away. Also there was no more sea. ² Then I, John, saw the holy city, New Jerusalem, coming down out of heaven from God, prepared as a bride adorned for her husband. ³ And I heard a loud voice from heaven saying, "Behold, the tabernacle of God is with men, and He will dwell with them, and they shall be His people. God Himself will be with them and be their God.* NKJV

What a Trip!

My husband Rog had already left for heaven but I had always wanted to drive the motor home to California. After long deliberation and some driving practice, I finally made plans, found two dear friends with adventurous spirits, and away we went. It was a glorious trip. I was so happy I had decided not to sell the RV. We saw Carlsbad Cavern and the Sonoma Desert and the Grand Canyon-we saw it all.

After a week and a half of sightseeing and immensely enjoying each other's company, we arrived at our destination- the breathtaking Pacific Ocean at Laguna Beach, California!

One evening, I parked the wonderful forty-foot motor home bulging with souvenirs and gifts for our families, and we ambled into a famous restaurant whose name I forget to celebrate our arrival. Supper was better than we could have imagined. When we were totally satiated with the stuff of this world we so enjoy, we left the restaurant and headed toward the RV, parked on a bluff on top of a low mountain overlooking the ocean.

We looked all around and couldn't locate the RV. I thought, *oh, no. Another senior moment! I can't remember where I parked it. And here we made it all the way to California with this scattered brain. What a miracle that was.*

It is never hard to find it, standing out like a train engine above all the other vehicles, but this time we couldn't spot it. It took me a few minutes to grasp the fact it was gone! Had someone stolen it? I had it locked. We started expressing all the possibilities. Finally it dawned on me that it could have rolled down the mountain! Impossible as it seemed, it was the only realistic explanation, and it was time to check it out. I still couldn't spot it. It was nowhere in sight.

As God would have it, two men in a wrecker were within our vision, working to get a car hauled away from the parking lot. I ran over to them and told them our predicament. I was hoping they would let me ride in their wrecker down the mountain to find it, hopefully resting on an uphill slope nearby. No such luck. They took two bicycles off the back of the wrecker and sped off down the mountain, with me running frantically behind them while the girls stood waiting and praying on the former parking spot of the RV.

As I ran, I was watching for signs the RV had hit anything, but there was not a clue anywhere, and no frantic people were around screaming about a runaway motor home flying through their neighborhood. I hoped God had put it in a safe place and I'd find it waiting patiently for me to find it.

I stopped to catch my breath from time to time and talked with dog-walkers and such, but nobody had a clue. As I got closer to the bottom, I realized it was a gradual winding road going toward the beach, but there was not one rise in the entire road. How in the world could that big monster make it to the bottom without mowing down any houses? The road was banked, but still...I was so confused...and terrified that someone could have easily been killed! Only my guardian angel could have guided it down.

It was at least a mile to the ocean. The men made it down quickly, but it took me a while. As the road straightened out and the beach was before me, from high above the water, I saw what I had hoped I would never see.

There was the very top of the RV, satellite dish glowing in the sunset, skylights I rarely had seen, and the entire motor home was underwater! I couldn't even think. I sat down in the middle of the road in shock. People were standing nearby staring at it, and the wrecker men just shook their heads.

I thought, *Oh my. I guess I should have sold it after all. Too late now!* Going through my mind was the incredible task of drying it out. Could it be salvaged at all? I had three hundred recently published books in there I hadn't even sold or given away yet. All our gifts were in there. And the comfy mattress on that king-sized bed! I could never dry that out! Would it ever run? And how in the world could a wrecker even pull it out?

I wondered if by some miracle it was airtight enough to be dry inside. Nothing is impossible with God. After all, if He could get it safely down that mountain, anything was possible.

Then instead of weeping, I got into hysterical laughing. *Rog is in heaven so he can't be angry at me. I have good insurance that will cover it all, and God took care of the difficult decision I was trying to make about parting with it... All is well that ends well. What I had considered a tragedy was just another amazing moment in my life. Who will ever believe this one?*

Then I woke up. Wow, what a relief it was to find I was dreaming!

Romans 8:28 NKJV *And we know that all things work together for good to those who love God, to those who are the called according to His purpose.*

Rapture

I had been listening to Merlin Carothers tapes on praising God in every situation. They were such a blessing.

At 5AM I woke up from this dream and just had to write it down the best I could remember it.

Carothers had offered a seminar in a large building, I think in Atlanta, on how to worship God. About 50,000 people showed up and stood in line waiting to get in, sort of like the lines at Brownsville during the revival. While they were waiting to get in, they began sharing with each other, and as they became united and loving on each other in Jesus, they began to be healed of all sorts of diseases, just like they often did at Brownsville. Crippled people were not in pain any more, and blind could begin to see 'men as trees walking', and the deaf could hear rumbling noises.

The doors opened and people filed in reverently, in wonder at the things that were beginning to happen. The healings continued and they were in awe. The audience consisted of all believers, of every color, size, shape and denomination. The only thing they had in common was Jesus Christ crucified and risen from the dead.

Merlin came out and the music started. Glory filled the place, and a rushing wind was swirling around. When they opened their mouths to sing, they all sang a common language, and it was not English!

The people were astounded at the Presence of God. Suddenly all in unison began floating toward the ceiling, and then I knew we were being raptured! I called Roger on my cell phone and told him what was happening, and that this was just the beginning. It was to be a preview of the worldwide rapture and soon we would be united again. The cell phone cut off, and as we reached the ceiling, everyone's clothing turned pure white- without spot or wrinkle- as brilliant as the sun. Halos or lights were visible on heads. We flowed right through the roof, and headed off to eternity, healed, delivered, and filled with God's Spirit. It wasn't in a twinkling of an eye, however, and it was in full view of anyone who was looking, or so it seemed.

I wonder how many times God has given a sample of something in the Bible before He did the big event. He raptured Enoch and Elijah, He opened graves at his crucifixion, He filled seventy with the Holy Ghost before Pentecost, and Jesus was transfigured on the mountain in front of two or three disciples. His clothes began to glow like in my dream. Can you think of any other things God did that He is going to do again?

1 Thessalonians 4:15-18 (KJV) *For this we say unto you by the word of the Lord, that we which are alive and remain unto the coming of the Lord shall not prevent them which are asleep.* [16] *For the Lord himself shall descend from heaven with a shout, with the voice of the archangel, and with the trump of God: and the dead in Christ shall rise first:* [17] *Then we which are alive and remain shall be caught up together with them in the clouds, to meet the Lord in the air: and so shall we ever be with the Lord.* [18] *Wherefore comfort one another with these words.*

1 Corinthians 15: (KJV) [44] *It is sown a natural body; it is raised a spiritual body. There is a natural body, and there is a spiritual body.* [50] *Now this I say, brethren, that flesh and blood* *cannot inherit the kingdom of God; neither doth corruption inherit incorruption. ⁵¹ Behold, I shew you a mystery; We shall not all sleep, but we shall all be changed, ⁵² In a moment, in the twinkling of an eye, at the last trump: for the trumpet shall sound, and the dead shall be raised incorruptible, and we shall be changed.*

⁵³ For this corruptible must put on incorruption, and this mortal must put on immortality. ⁵⁴ So when this corruptible shall have put on incorruption, and this mortal shall have put on immortality, then shall be brought to pass the saying that is written, Death is swallowed up in victory.

Matthew 24:42-44 (KJV) *Watch therefore: for ye know not what hour your Lord doth come. ⁴³ But know this, that if the goodman of the house had known in what watch the thief would come, he would have watched, and would not have suffered his house to be broken up. ⁴⁴ Therefore be ye also ready: for in such an hour as ye think not the Son of man cometh.*

Last Chance

I woke up from what I would call a nightmare. My heart was beating like a drum, and I couldn't return to sleep. I had to write this down. It may be close to the truth.

I was in a place in which several heathen people were being held. They had refused to believe the Bible or what God said to the entire world. They were given one more chance to hear. They were each placed in a confined area, all in a row, and divided into small groups, about five in a row. Each row was then pressed flat and set standing up into a device that held them in place, sort of like pressing chicken pieces and laying them next to each other in a bag. Each were then stood upright and put in standup layers, sort of like pages in a book, into what appeared to be a big freezer. Before the door was shut, they were told the message of the gospel.

They were told that if they would believe what was being taught them while they stood there unable to resist or speak, they would be saved and even after they froze to death, they would wake up in heaven. If not, they would wake up in hell.

They were told after they heard the message, the door would be opened one more time, and those that had not yet died would hear the message one more time. Then if they refused to believe, they would be lost forever and no one could save or help them. All I could think of was, *I wonder how long they can last before they have no air.*

The message told to them while they were unable to argue was this:

Romans 3:23. *All have sinned and come short of the glory of God.* (Every single soul ever born has sinned. Not one has the right to stand before a Holy God and enter His eternal place.)

Romans 6:23 *For the wages of sin is death; but the gift of God is eternal life through Jesus Christ our Lord.*

Romans 5:8-9 *Christ Jesus died while we were yet sinners, to save us with His shed blood. His blood washes us white as snow.*

Confess with your mouth the Lord Jesus and believe in your heart that God has raised Him from the dead you will be saved. ^{10} For with the heart one believes unto righteousness, and with the mouth confession is made unto salvation.
Romans 10:9-10 *But God demonstrates His own love toward us, in that while we were still sinners, Christ died for us. ^{9} Much more then, having now been justified by His blood, we shall be saved from wrath through Him.*
Romans 5:8, 9 *If we confess our sins, He is faithful and just to forgive us our sins and to cleanse us from all unrighteousness.*
I John 1:9 *Therefore, having been justified by faith, we have peace with God through our Lord Jesus Christ...*
Romans 5:1 *Jesus said, "I go to prepare a place for you, that where I am you will be also."*

    The pressure they were under had a purpose, to get their attention so they would focus on what was important and stop running to and fro doing what they wanted. They were forced to listen in hopes of saving even one.

    Then the freezer door swung slowly shut. Their eyes were wide open. They couldn't speak but only listen. Some were too scared even to hear. Their minds were racing and they knew they may die, but each held out some insane hope that he alone would make it. These had their minds on their possessions that were being lost, and not on the fact their souls were being tested. They were not paying attention, and they would not survive spiritually or physically.

This was a symbolic dream. I can imagine this is what God would like to do, but He gave us free will. Recently the Holy Spirit had told me time was nearly gone. It was time to woo them no longer, but tell them plainly in hopes of saving some. He said to preach it in and out of season, because there isn't much time. The devil has come to earth and knows his time is short, and he will make lives miserable.

God sent His Son to save us from the tricks of the devil, and to purchase our souls from him using the blood of Jesus as payment. No other payment will do.

We can surrender completely to Him. We cannot trust in our own good deeds, because all of them have a selfish purpose. Every heart is wicked. Nobody is perfect to stand before God. God will protect our souls from hell. We will live forever.

Some end up in prison before they will search for or respond to God. Some continue to try and satisfy their desires with earthly things instead of seeking to let God satisfy them.

The Word of God is sharper than a two-edged sword, able to divide the soul from the spirit. Only God's Word is able to set us free from bondage. Counselors can't do it- only this sword.

Many people have come forward in a church or meeting and said they accepted Jesus as their Savior. But they must also believe in their hearts.

Our comfort is I John 4:15- "Whoever shall confess Jesus is the Son of God dwells in Him and he in God. The Message Bible *says Everyone who confesses that Jesus is God's Son participates continuously in an intimate relationship with God.*

A Peek into Tomorrow

It came upon us before we expected! We planned to store water and food and be together on the day it hit, but it came too early. We were not prepared for this! God said nobody would know the day or the hour. We figured it would be later rather than earlier than when we thought it would.

My husband Rog and I were at Dave Underwood's in Grand Rapids, Michigan, looking out the window. His mom, Sadie, was with us. Suddenly the sun went out- for just a split second. I was the only one who saw it. Nobody paid attention. They figured my eyes were playing tricks on me. I don't blame them. So did I!

Then the earth quivered beneath my feet- just for a tiny speck of time. They all thought they had noticed it, too, but again it was so quick. We went back to visiting. I kept an eye out for the sun. "There! It went out again! Didn't anybody notice it?"

"No. You need to get your eyes tested, Jude," said Shayne.

We went on a tour of their gorgeous home. It had everything you could possibly ever need or want! We went to the kitchen and sat down for a cup of coffee. Shayne poured my cup. I was peering into it, and it saw a small ripple form in the cup. I had not touched it. My nerves began to tingle. I knew that I knew that God was doing something, or the earth was having birth pangs. Nobody noticed but me, but I had read enough to know it was going to happen one day…and this may be the day. Adrenalin sped up my heart rate. I didn't know how to convince them. I suddenly forgot every Bible verse that told about it. How I wished I had taken a list of events with me! I could see I would not be able to convince anyone what was happening until it got severe!

There went the sun again. This time the darkness lasted long enough they should have seen the difference. I said it again. Instead they decided something better be done with me. Shayne got me a Tylenol! She mentioned something about visual migraines. "Shayne! You know the Bible."

"I know we will be raptured before the tribulation," she said. "You read too many books."

I went upstairs to their bathroom, and filled the sink with water. Then I went around searching for a Bible. None could be found. How I wished I had retained what I knew. I wished I had been prepared farther ahead, and that I was with my family right now.

It began to rain, slowly at first, then the sky simply opened up, and we had a downpour like I have never seen- a real gully-washer! No warning. Just like that! It got pitch black for about a minute. We turned on the lights. Nobody panicked but me.

I started praying silently in the spirit, and asked Jesus what I should be doing next. The ground trembled….just for a second. Everyone's eyes got larger than usual. It was getting their attention.

When the big quake started, it felt like a dog shaking a rag doll in his mouth, and we were the rag dolls. I was tossed from the couch to the chair on the other side of the room as though an invisible hand had picked me up and thrown me! Part of the roof must have split, because we heard a deafening shredding sound! Water seeped down into the living room. Shayne ran for anything plastic to cover expensive pieces of furniture. They were paying attention now. None of us knew what to do next. I went to fill the bathtubs with water. All the children were up and in the kitchen by now, trembling in their pajamas. The sun was back, but it was very dim. The lights were still working but I knew they would soon be out.

The most horrible part was that my kids were not close by. I wondered if they had felt it. I tried to call, but the phones were already out. Another trembling of the earth brought us all to our knees. Would you not think we all would have prayed? Instead we tried to think of what to do next! Old habits die hard!

The light outside was now coming in flashes. We all ran for the windows. It appeared that the sun was dancing! Huge brilliant flashes rose way up in the sky, first in the east, and a second later in the west. It looked like a vast display of orange fireworks that had all gone off at once! It was clearly visible even through the downpour.

All I could think of was our kids, and how to get to them. We had to make it out somehow. Rog felt the same way. Whatever it took, we had to get there. But first we had to get to Holland to check on Mom and our other families. Against great opposition, especially from Dave's mom Sadie, we got in the car, with big glasses of water from the tub, threw in whatever stuff we had, and our shoes. Away we went, telling them to find a Bible and read Matthew 24. ..and pray for safety and provision.

The roads were miraculously intact. Everyone seemed to be in shock yet, so the roads

were not jammed. But it would not be long. How I wished I had recalled the next event to come!
 I woke up, and started saving milk jugs!

1 Thessalonians 5:1-2 New King James Version
But concerning the times and the seasons, brethren, you have no need that I should write to you. ² For you yourselves know perfectly that the day of the Lord so comes as a thief in the night.

The Green Men
What can this mean?

It seems I owned a restaurant that looked like a house, and I lived in it as well. A large group of friends came over and we had a wonderful prayer meeting. During the meeting, some of us actually rose up from the floor (like Elijah?) and found ourselves nearly at the ceiling, worshiping God. There were small clusters of us, holding hands or hugging, and we had floated upward, but gradually landed gently on the ground again. I recalled the words "lifted up" and decided I better study those words later.

We had a glorious time. A few people left, not understanding what was going on, and were probably afraid. Gradually everyone left, and I was alone with a few folks who worked their way to a lower level to visit. I had with me a child and a baby.

After a while, a small group of Orientals, two men and a woman came to the front door and simply walked in without knocking, though I was not open at the time. I tried to explain it, but they acted like they didn't understand. I asked if they were hungry, but nobody answered. The woman walked right into the kitchen, pulled out my huge pans, and started cooking a large amount of food she had with her. I didn't know what to do. I just stood there watching as she took over my kitchen, cooking tomatoes and other strange things. The men made themselves at home, turned on the TV and took most of their clothes off, like they were in their own home relaxing. They all acted like I was invisible and completely ignored me.

I started looking around for my cell phone but it was not where it had been. I got the children and went to the lower level where friends were still hanging around. I tried to tell them something weird was going on, but they were not alarmed, nor would they call the police or go for help. I sensed we were being invaded in some way, but this was something very unfamiliar. I didn't know how to cope with it.

I seemed to be most responsible for the baby, about two years old. I put the baby on my back, took my purse, and went outside to a neighbor. I headed down the street, and there were two men dressed in green uniforms, armed, in front of one neighbor's house,

I headed the opposite direction, and two more green men were stationed in front of another house. So I slowly retreated and got into a van in our yard, looking for a cell phone or something with which to call the police. I found nothing. Going back to the lower level of the house, I again tried to warn my friends. By then, they were aware something was going on none of us understood. Some group that was well organized was invading us and already the area was under siege.

I got to my laptop computer and wrote a letter to send to all my Email addresses, but knew nobody would believe such a preposterous story. Besides that, what individual would act on it alone? What could I say that would cause them to take action? What action could anyone take?

If this really happened, we are such greenhorns about combat and being prisoners, we have no clue how to respond. Even if our government knew this was possible, how could they train us without bringing panic and bedlam to the nation?

We have a few ways to deal with natural disasters, but how would we deal with enemies from within like this? One clue was in the first part of the dream. Get together and pray! Find out how to fly, like we seemed able to do when we were 'in the Spirit.'

This would be the time to get our faith strong as possible, practicing doing the Word of God, and finding out what kind of deeds could be done that are "greater than I have done", as Jesus said. This is our best defense.

Imagine if we were actually able to worship God and when it got dark, simply float away! Wouldn't that spook our enemy!

1 Thessalonians 4:17 (NKJV) *Then we who are alive and remain shall be caught up together with them in the clouds to meet the Lord in the air. And thus we shall always be with the Lord.*

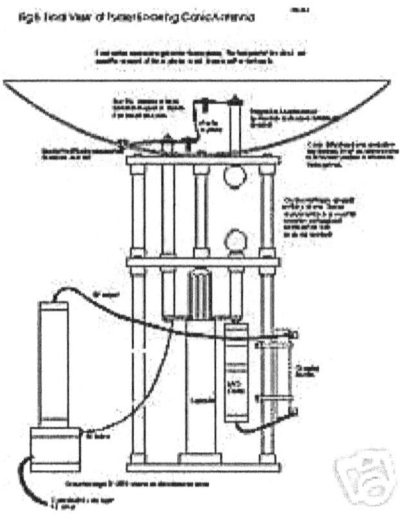

An EMP Dream

We were at a conference in a hotel, and the motorhome we used to get there was parked in the huge lot nearby. For some reason we had slept in the hotel. My friend Donna from California was with me.

Breakfast had just been served when suddenly all the lights went out. Hundreds of us just sat there sort of stunned as after several minutes, no announcements were made. The backup power system had not clicked on as we expected. Pretty soon the news trickled through the room that we had been hit by an EMP! "The power is out and the entire city is dead," someone in the crowd said. That profound statement soared like a bullet from one end of the room to the other.

Donna and I decided to find the RV and decide what to do next. The room was pitch black. All we had was a dim memory of how to get out of there.

We saw a tiny light far away from us where a door was open. The crowd was pouring out of it like water from a pitcher. As we wove our way toward the light we heard snatches of animated conversation.

"What caused the blackout? Why didn't a generator start and give them power?" Speculations increased the din until we sounded like a hoard of bees in a busy hive. All I could remember hearing about electromagnetic pulses was that it has been predicted that a single high altitude burst 200 miles above Kansas could propagate an EMP enveloping the entire United States. I imagined living without power and reverting America to pioneer days. My heart started racing, waking me up.

***

Two amazing things that made me write this were that I had never heard of an EMP in 1984. Also the next day after I woke from the dream our power was off when I got up! How could I have a dream that came true that very day? An ice storm in the night had broken power lines in the area. We ended up without power for a whole week! Thank God, we had a fireplace and plenty wood, a freezer that kept food cold all week because the house was freezing, and we had plenty food to last all week. We were stuck sleeping all over the family room, eating and cooking in there, like campers in a cave. I do not recall not having water, so the faucets must have worked.

The reason I remember it so well is that we had a newborn granddaughter and her family living with us. The baby got pneumonia and was brought to the hospital, where she died three days later. Yes, I will always remember that storm.

I read about EMPs several years later. This is a short excerpt. Wikipedia: An **electromagnetic pulse** (sometimes abbreviated **EMP**) is a burst of electromagnetic radiation that results from an explosion (usually from the detonation of a nuclear weapon) and/or a suddenly fluctuating magnetic field. The resulting rapidly changing electric fields or magnetic fields may couple with electrical/electronic systems to produce damaging current and voltage surges. You can read about it online.

Visions

I saw a mountain with people of all beliefs at different heights and positions on the mountain. Those climbing got closer to each other and closer to God the higher they went.

God gave me a verse in Ephesians 4:12, 13 He gave us people to help us mature until we believe alike about Jesus and salvation and are filled full with Christ.

***

I saw a huge hourglass shortly after the baptism in the Holy Spirit. I was leaning down from the narrow neck at the center, trying to encourage others to come up higher where there was safety, but nobody paid attention. Suddenly they seemed to know of danger below, and all of them tried to come higher at once, but they would not fit through the narrow opening together, and many fell backward.

I had been saved since Thanksgiving. On my first Easter morning, I woke to see in the spirit, total darkness. Then in the left side of my eye, I began to see a sliver of light pushing the darkness away. The light continued to shove the darkness from left to right until the entire vision was simply a brilliant light. Then I understand that Jesus came to destroy the darkness, and that was what Easter was all about.

***

God showed me a wonderful miracle. I saw a vision of our two older sons sitting at a small table, studying the Bible together. At that time, this was an impossibility, but recently it came to pass!

***

My friend Carol had a vision of long tables filled with rotten vegetables as far as you could see. People were grabbing and stepping on each other to take them. Suddenly the sky split open, and Jesus appeared in the sky. Some of the people began floating upward.

***

Before he married again, our son Dave had a vision of him rising with his children to meet Jesus in the air. His friends were left behind.

***

Marilyn Kolean was at our Bible study when she saw the word "Baptism" in red letters. Shortly after that, Jesus baptized me in the Holy Ghost.

***

Lois was saved when Jesus showed her a vision of Him hanging on the cross, and His blood was falling on the ground and all over her. She said it was as if she was there in the flesh.

***

Tom Papania saw a light in his prison cell and Jesus told him of his ministry unfolding. He is now an evangelist with a powerful testimony.

***

Carolyn smoked marijuana for 25 years. One night she gave her life to God. A few nights later she was smoking dope, and told God she thought He had taken the desire away. Suddenly her heart started racing like she was having a heart attack! She began racing around, and realized there were beings in the room with her. She was terrified. Then the Holy Spirit spoke to her and said, "Get a garbage bag and throw all the garbage in it. It is all garbage!" Once she finally did it, just as quickly as it came, her heart slowed to a normal pace. That was the last time she smoked marijuana, and she had no trouble with it since. That was 1996.

***

Melissa sees visions on a regular basis. It seems to be the way God communicates with her. Her life is unique, but she overcame a great deal of pain and conflict before God redeemed it.

"I had committed to this little book of prayer for thirty days. That was on the 14th day, about two weeks into this book. I hit my knees after a visitor left. I recited the prayer. I've never forgotten it. "Holy Spirit, I know thou art indwelling me. I know that Jesus has arisen and ascended to heaven. I know thou art come to be my constant companion and guide. Speak to me and guide me now." That was the key! Boy, did He speak!

I saw the Lord with a white cloak and blue sash draped across Him. He had a rod or staff in His hand. It was the most beautiful sight I had ever seen. He came in the vision with the Shekinah glory. The colors were beautiful beyond description and I saw angels encircling around Him. Then He stepped forward and I saw a lamb at His side.

A rainbow appeared behind Him as He began to speak to me, saying, "Melissa, they call you Lisa, but I call you by your name because I named you Melissa Ruth. I have come to tell you that it is true. What you're seeing is real. I am real, and I love you and have great plans for you and your great life. Trust Me and know that I'm working everything out for you. Just remember that I love you. Never forget this, because I will come back and visit with you soon."

I suddenly saw a lion at his side and the lamb that He had picked up and held He put down to walk. He walked away with the lion and the lamb. Then I saw the angels come closer. They were circling in front of me.

I said, "Please don't go!" I didn't want Him to leave. That was the most gorgeous sight I had ever seen. I was mesmerized for weeks after that vision. I had never seen anything like that! I had tapped on the door of heaven and Jesus had answered! What a concept! I had never known Jesus on a personal level or what was meant by a lion and a lamb! I just knew it was so wonderful and so real. I saw His hands and I will never forget that. I could see the nail scars but blinding gold lined in red like blood radiated off the holes in his hands.

It blew my mind. I had never even thought about that until I saw it for myself. I became very sad because He was leaving. The angels around me said, "Don't cry and don't be sad. This is real and you can talk to Him any time."

The Lord told me that he had chosen me for His purpose. I didn't understand. I really didn't even know any Bible stories much less how to be used and see visions from God. I had no idea about the prophetic gifts.

Satan attacked me at an early age because of the call on my life. I know that now, but I didn't have any idea that the enemy wants to keep us unaware of who we are. When we realize it, we are still blinded by the WHO being our DO. I mean by that, who we are is never based on what we do. That's an old snare of the enemy. He has no new tricks. He uses the same old plans to keep us under pressure to DO and gradually it becomes normal for us.

Melissa Patterson has written an amazing book called, "His Story through a Seer's Eyes. It is available on Amazon.com and Kindle.

Message from the Holy Spirit

Let not your hearts be troubled. Believe in me and I shall give you the morning star. Trust me with all your hearts and I will reveal myself to you. You are not set aside to be pummeled by the enemy, though it feels that way for the moment. The troubles of the moment are temporary but the joy of the Lord is your strength. Nothing shall by any means harm, your spirit. Your body is another matter, as you already know. This body is part of this world and it shall not go with you when I come for you. It is dying daily but your spirit is safe. Nothing can by any means harm it. Did you think your body would never have pain? Did I promise you a rose garden? I promised I would be with you in troubles and tribulation and that I have overcome the world.

There is nothing in this world that can snatch you out of my hand except your own will. I never remove free will from you. You shall use it until you are overtaken by death or My appearance.

About Visions

The book of Joel describes things to occur in the last days. "And it shall come to pass in the last days, saith God, I will pour out of my Spirit upon all flesh: and your sons and your daughters shall prophesy, and your young men shall see visions, and your old men shall dream dreams."

Corporeal vision is a <u>supernatural</u> manifestation of an object to the eyes of the body. Imaginative vision is the sensible representation of an object by the act of <u>imagination</u> alone, without the aid of the visual organ. Intellectual visions perceive the object without a sensible image.

The End...for now.

Bibliography

Judy Parrott has a passion to help precious souls find and enjoy a relationship with their Creator through God's Son Jesus. They are available at Amazon.com and on Kindle. She married her sweetheart Roger who went to live with Jesus in 2010 after 53 years of marriage. They share three sons, eight grandchildren and five great grandchildren. She shared the gospel over the years with the Christian Motorcyclists Association, teaches Sunday school, and has volunteered with several organizations. Judy worked years ago as a nurse and has an associate seminary degree. Jesus Christ is the most important person in her life.

"Mysterious Wonders" records forty amazing miraculous events that cannot be forgotten by the world. God said to tell the world of His wonderful deeds. These are truly wonderful.

"Break Every Chain" is a book of addiction recovery stories with guidelines, scientific information and spiritual revelations resulting from her family experiences. Love is the greatest force in the world. It sets captives free from any addiction.

"A Life Worth Living" is an autobiography. Walk with me through my life stories. As with every life, they are unique and worthy to be shared as entertainment and lessons I learned, most of them the hard way.

Tribute to Roger Emmett Parrott

As the editor and author of the book, Amazing Moments, I was invited to write a tribute to my precious husband, who passed away Sunday morning, March 21, 2010, after a violent but courageous battle against diabetes, kidney disease, anemia, and congestive heart failure. He left me behind to nurture a bunch of people, three sons and wives, eight grandkids and four and a half great grandkids. He won only because Jesus Christ lived in his heart and when his last enemy, death, tried to conquer him, Jesus took him home forever.

Roger was a wonderful provider with great integrity, determination, and faith. We had a good life for 53 years, and I have no regrets. He worked his way up to become the Southern Operations Director of Herman Miller Furniture Company, and after 36 years, he retired, and passed on to heaven at 72. He had been the president of the North Fulton Chamber of Commerce. He loved traveling, motorcycling, hunting, fishing, RV's...and later on, napping, napping.... and more napping.

With ticket in hand, Rog caught the heavenly train Sunday morning at 9:39 AM. I saw him before he left, in a dream. He was in restraints, but figured a way to reach his ventilator and pull it out! He had been unable to breathe without it for eight days, and he found out he could breathe after yanking it out! He was running and talking and full of joy. I woke up and got dressed to go tell him about the dream.

I got in the car, and remembered my cell phone back in the house. I ran back to get it and the phone rang. Diedre, the nurse, told me his heart was growing weak and irregular, and his blood pressure was falling. I drove the ten miles at record speed, but he left his body one-half a minute before I got in the room to say goodbye. He left without a struggle. I know my dream came true for him that moment. He did everything he wanted to do in this life and he finally got his reward. We will rejoice for him and mourn our loss.

He is safe in the arms of Jesus, and enjoying the reunion with those he loves. Thank you for letting me share.

Judy Parrott

©All Rights Reserved. 2015
Heavens Hands Publications

Made in the USA
Columbia, SC
09 September 2020